Retail Arbitrage in 2019

Table of Contents

Introduction 1

Chapter 1: Introduction to Retail Arbitrage 2

    Market Affiliation 6

Chapter 2: The Advantages of Retail Arbitrage 9

    Budget Dynamics 13

    Need Low Budget for Starters 14

    Easy to Get Started 15

    Easy to Scale-Up 17

Chapter 3: Retail Arbitrage in the Modern Approach 19

    "Tactical Arbitrage" 20

    The Approach of "Online Arbitrage" 22

    Product Diversity 25

Chapter 4: All Ways to Do Retail Arbitrage 28

    Amazon 29

    eBay 30

Private Labeling 33

Multi-Channel Fulfillment 35

Chapter 5: Researching and Choosing the Right Product 37

Where and How to Find the Right Products 42

Where to Buy the Right Items to Sell at High Margin 44

Chapter 6: What is the FBA Process and How Does it Work? 49

Rules of the Amazon marketplace 50

The FBA System 51

The Approach of the FBA System to Retail Arbitrage 54

Chapter 7: How to Sell Products with the FBA System 59

Chapter 8: Scaling Up Your FBA Business 72

Methods for Obtaining Reviews 75

Move into Wholesale 76

Move into Private Labeling 78

Advertise the Products 81

Use the Multi-Channel Fulfillment System 92

Reminders... 110

Chapter 9: Get Started with Retail Arbitrage 116

Revenue Tracking 134

Profit Banqueting 138

Recap 142

Conclusion 145

Introduction

This book will talk about a practical approach to Retail Arbitrage in our age. It will explain every single step, the process, benefits, and downfalls. Retail Arbitrage or Online Arbitrage (OA) is a way of selling common goods that are marked down for remarketing to other sources at different rates. Through OA, sales are going to be made faster and they are going to take a more automated spin for each sale. This is going to create a strong presence for the company, whether it is on their social media or with other partners that hold hands in these partner sales. Exclusive sales are going to be made with OA, and this could create a powerful routine and mission statement that will follow the sale from the distributor to the warehouses and to the customer. Dive into this book with the rights to earn and let's make it something we can all participate in.

Chapter 1: Introduction to Retail Arbitrage

Retail arbitrage is a rising trend for all businesses making sales everywhere around the world. It is a trend to jump on and to profit in new ways for the selling shop, whether it is a physical shop or maybe an online retailer that is even dropshipping. Retail arbitrage is the movement of common goods or high-end goods that are purchased at a marked down rate, and these products are sold to many different customers from everywhere. These goods can be marked back up again to gain a profit for the merchant. This is going to be a good move for any wholesaling business that is already selling thousands of units at a time. Creating a formula that will profit the business with these selling moves is going to build a great selling source that is well-known for their good prices on items even if they don't seem like they are marked down. Retail arbitrage creates a safe selling field for any merchant that is looking to represent marked down items.

OA has been a central part of some companies up until this new generation is coming about, where more and more people are beginning to take on this new strategy and there are goods being sold everywhere. This is a train a lot of people are going to jump on just to get their taste of profit. It is possible to have a company that is solely running on selling retail arbitrage, but with this kind of structure, there is going to be a constant change in product line supply and demand. Sell as much as you choose, but remember that the company will be relying on the product popularity to decide what is going on the shelves for the month. The business may be making specific business ventures that involve dealing exclusively to certain companies. This could create an isolated market so it can be a good thing and a bad thing, but it must be monitored for every congruency so that the profits are going to match up at the end of the quarterly making. This kind of venture is going to be good for the company to have secured and dedicated buyers in the scene that are going to keep coming back for the regulars. It will be good for markets that are untapped and who don't want to be a break in the ice for other shops or marketers to come in and take the limelight. This type of venture can go south at times when there is such an isolated market that it is keeping the clients selective. If the clients are not sufficient for the company to be making a high earning, then we need to broaden the focus for more clients. There needs to be adequate revenue coming in for the business to do more than just breakeven in the shop. If there needs to be another client, we need to reach out and use the same formulas we have made to make the progress with the companies we are with.

Move correctly to keep your market flowing and abundant. It is okay to have an abundant market reach for brands that are unpopular and popular alike. This is going to become a safety net to have more clients and brand advertisement. Having a high population client base is going to create more brand awareness, that is going to generate consistent revenue and keep a strong structure for the future sales that the company shop will be making. With retail arbitrage, there is going to be an adjustment in the selling market for new products and new pricing. New products always come out with a new price when other competing products are released and sold at a lower value. When competing companies release products close to each other in release dates, there tends to be a falsified value that skews the market. Skewing the market is going to adjust the quarterly profits for the other companies because they are going to be making up for sales lost that was toward a cheaper market. Cheaper markets make low-quality items and they sell them at almost full retail price because of the release of the product. With retail arbitrage, skewing the market becomes easier and easier when the consumer themselves forget about the true product value.

Market Affiliation

Marketing through company affiliation is one of the strongest ways to begin selling company products and receiving residual income by accruing interest that the company gives just for representing the product brand. It is not the easiest to become a company affiliate marketer because there have to be many pieces of the puzzle to put together. There needs to be an IEN number for example and the business would benefit from being listed with a bank. There are other things like setting up the bank account correctly for financial tracking purposes. Affiliate marketing is going to pay off more and more if the company becomes a close source to the brand. By doing this, the company will need to have proper social exposure and efficient traffic to the site so that there is product awareness and there won't be time wasted on sites that are not selling or bringing in customers. Unlike other means of representing other company brands that involve buying the copyright to the brand, the company will have to just initiate themselves into the brand affiliation and apply on their affiliate forms. This is typically not the easiest process for most companies because the verification process can be strenuous. There are many factors that come in, like company shop exposure and brand representation. A wealthy company is going to expect the advising company to have a strong presence as well and to not waste their time in these engagements.

Market affiliation will offer incentive packs to the company shops marketing with interest revenues that are made by every product that is sold and the company shop will receive a percentage of the sale. This may not be one of the best interest rates, but at the rate of an independent wholesaler, these products can make profits if it is all done correctly. If a company wholesales 5,000 units of a well-known brand once they become an affiliate marketer, then the interest rate on the products is going to be very good for the selling shop considering they are receiving exponential revenue from selling products that have different brandings. The rate for market affiliation is anywhere from 0.05% to 0.1% interest rates on any sales being made for the affiliate brand and the company will be rewarded for representing them on the site. Get the most out of this program by selling wholesale capacity retail arbitrage and making the strong formula for ultimate profits.

Chapter 2: The Advantages of Retail Arbitrage

The thresholding for startup costs is quite low in this day and age, unlike any other retail business. And of the great parts about it is that there are companies that support other companies and their selling and dropshipping businesses. It is relatively simple to jump into this stream and sell on sites without even a subscription fee. The companies that support other dropshippers will receive a cut from the profits but they will be in good standing with these companies, like for example, Amazon. Companies like Amazon help other businesses progress through their business expanding, also considering high web traffic and high buyer rates. The great reputations will be a great base for the distributors with their shops of retail arbitrage flowing and it will also be a great reputation to uphold. Orders are going to be fulfilled properly for every customer and they will have to meet a certain standard to be processed and shipped. We haven't talked about the product yet so we have to consider manufacturers when we consider using these extra sources to help us create product revenue. Retail arbitrage can be easier when used through a system and through a formula.

There have to be healthy ROI rates in order for them to carry over profits for the company. Mind this that ROI and net profit are two different worlds and you cannot call these two the same thing. On FBA sites that assist companies in their dropshipping, duties often have rules and fees. Items that typically sell for anything less than $20 will usually have fees of $4.01, which will also be a package that is under 2 pounds. Then you must add the 15% fee or $3 for the $20 dollar item that is being listed, which if that item cost you only $10 dollars, then through the purchase, the company will have made a margin of 2.99 and the ROI of this would be 30%.

There has to be a reasonable balance between purchases by volume and by margin because there are going to be markets to hold for consistent sales. Some sales are going to be supplied through means of a high volume of buyers visiting the source for many common goods or necessities perhaps, or there is going to be sales driven by marginal profits made to keep sales from wavering and a constant stream of buyer traffic to the shop. The company needs to keep a steady stream of incoming traffic for there to be strong numbers through the profits. The fees will help the profit breakeven for every purchase as long as there is a good price set for the product. There can be a gray zone for the price zone and it can make or break the company's chances of getting the sale over another company that has the same products. This is going to come when the company is deciding on what products to purchase and having a stable sourcing supplier that is going to be dedicated through their selling adventures. Depending on the size and the weight of the product that is being shipped, these FBA policies are going to apply under different rates and charge accordingly on a fixed process. It may be efficient to have a product that is a good proportionate weight to the price point of the product and otherwise will cut into the listing price, which could also result in higher profits earned. This should be strategically handled with a formula that is meant for handling profit revenue and marginal income for the shop. With arbitrage restocking, certain shelves for products is going to come with its setbacks if the company is selling a product that is not popular, but once the company takes a deeper dive into spending more money on better quality items, they are going to find it easier to sell in massive quantities and make consistent sales from selling the same items. There is an important niche to go with the trends at times, but other times it is going to be profitable to sell the same items once the company recognized the impact it is making to their monthly revenue. Find the right product to sell and it will make the fees and regulations easier to abide by with these selling systems. There needs to be an economic standpoint taken when considering what the right product will be when you are selling these items, and that is why companies like Amazon through FBA give lists of several products to choose from. These products range from home décor to auto shop appliances, and there could be many avenues taken as the suppliers are ready to stock by the thousands.

Budget Dynamics

Through basic retail arbitrage, the company will be able to list products at a marked down cost and make a great profit off of distinctive sales made on other platforms through different means. These sale strategies could range anywhere from personal investment sales that could be exclusive or to other distributors or companies that are trying to get a better deal on their bulk buying. There are budget dynamics that need to be made at the beginning of the purchases and all profits need to be formulated before there is a leap of money to be dropped on new inventories. These budget dynamics are going to be formulated depending on the current product that is being distributed and at what rate there will be selling these products. To list more products, it could be an extra charge for the space in the market and this will also have to be a factor to think about if the company is selling one thousand items or even ten thousand items. Keep a good track of every dollar spent and make sure it is going to the right accounts for the right purposes.

Need Low Budget for Starters

There is going to be a great entry budget for selling retail arbitrage considering that you can generate revenue with a good product that can make you consistent income to maintain revenue growth. A company can start gaining profits with a $300 budget and they will be able to make more moves with their startup costs. If the company is purchasing 100 pieces of inventory to flip for their customers, then the profits they receive from these units will be able to generate revenue for the company to then get 150 units for the next quarter. This will increase until the company has reached 1000% capacity of their original inventory plane. Once the company begins to sell 1000 units and then 1500 units of the inventory, the company will begin to receive extra revenues and dividends for the extra inventory that is making its way to racking up on the online shelves. Extra inventory is going to lead to extra sales and special events.

Easy to Get Started

This is an easy process to get going as long as there are an initial money budget and a general focus to where the company's motives are going to be made. The company is going to need to do product research and have a firm grasp of their product market and what crowds are going to be sold to for maximum exposure. The company may have to expand on other products or begin dropshipping other products if there is a change in the trending topics, or if the product takes revenue cuts through production manifesting. There is going to be a lot of hard work initially for these works, and it is necessary to find oneself going the extra miles to satisfy the customers that are being dropshipped to. Branching out to find new clients is going to be a crucial part of finding a great niche in the scene that has dedicated buyers. Find a great product that isn't going to be falling off of the sales graphs any time soon, and if it is a common good, then there can be a continuous fan base built on the same values. Online shoppers everywhere are looking for fast and convenient shipping which is a great pride Amazon can take part in. Amazon offers a lot of perks to not only their customers but the businesses that are scaling up with them. Through Amazon fulfillment services, companies are able to meet high standards by shipping and handling high product loads for customers that are in need around the world. They take out the huge stress of managing inventory and create simple means to get products to the customers. With these services, it gives everyone a chance to become a part of the revolutionizing change in e-commerce. Anyone can use these services whether they are selling goods every day for a living, or if they are leaving college and trying to get rid of extra things that can be marked down. OA is already going to be marked down so the simplicity of creating profits from sourced items is going to be easy once the right formula for ROI and price count is established.

Easy to Scale-Up

Scaling up with retail arbitrage is going to be determined on the amount of drive and money that is put into the shops reach. There is going to be a possible gate on the amount of inventory that needs to be purchased, but as long as the company scales up with the products and proportions that are manageable to the company, the structure will be figured in a strong manner. There needs to be a threshold made between the number of products that are being purchased and the annual ROI, which can keep good standing with the margins that are earned every quarter. Lower ROI is going to create great progress for any company that is trying to make a set goal of profit in a fixed amount of time. Other processes can be made by purchasing many different products with different ROI's, and this is going to create a more diverse profit field which could be more high-end.

Chapter 3: Retail Arbitrage in the Modern Approach

When beginning selling retail arbitrage, there are going to be plenty of rates for the products that you can flip. These rates are going to range from the companies being suppliers and some being demanders. The basic jest is that the company will purchase products from 3rd party sites that are different or lower prices than the same items on Amazon. When the company lists these items, they can generate the profit from the fixed pricing. The key for the company after their first sales is to reinvest all of the funds back into the business to ramp up production, and soon the mere one hundred dollar investment can surely turn into a thousand dollar investment with the right type of work ethic and exposure.

"Tactical Arbitrage"

One of the things that need to be obtained is a tool for product browsing. There are tools like Tactical Arbitrage and this tool is going to browse hundreds of online sites so that you can find a product that is low priced and even lower than Amazon. Tools like Tactical Arbitrage have systems that can generate leads for the owner while they are engaged in other activities or rather in the background. With this tool or other tools alike, you can easily set your own ROIs and sales ranks for products that will sell fast and easily as you are searching these sites for great products. This tool is also going to be used to link wholesales accounts into the mix, as there will be purchasing from these parties as well comparatively with their pricings listed alongside Amazon. A great way to check out product popularity for revenue formulation is a tool inside that is called ASIN Variation Analysis, and this is going to display which items are selling anywhere from clothes to dining kitchenware. The tool will cost the budget, but it is a reasonable price ranging anywhere from $70 to $150 for the whole package on an account and there can be many advantages taken. Filter your data to find any product that is on the site and find anywhere to minimums of 20% ROI for the products that are going to be bulked as well. This tool is great for a company that needs to change up their product selections or maybe a company that is picking their first products to a great beginning to their new shop. If a company wanted to try it out to see if it's a fit for them, they have a 7-day free trial on their company website and after that, they can easily upgrade to the Full Suite package that is going to include wholesale, Amazon flips and their vast library search each month.

The Approach of "Online Arbitrage"

The approach of online retail arbitrage is coming fast and anyone with a computer can jump aboard and see what it can do for them. There are going to be a lot of companies that are looking for the same goals to meet, but there are only going to be strong companies in the market that hold their strong footing in their community to keep revenue flowing. Once the product is chosen, the company is going to send their shipping sales to a prep center which makes it way easier to expand the business with every move. There are typically extra supplies mind you so that there can be other dropshipping sales made if the company is focusing only on wholesaling. Find a product and study its details and its dimensions. While you are on the search, you can even download a free program that is called Keepa and it is an extension that is installed to show you vital information that will be helping you make great buying decisions. With Keepa, you can check the average sales rakes and the total number of sellers that are representing the product. Scan the products with the tools we have been talking about to determine a product's profitability and this will simulate what the FBA system will also do. The FBA system provides a Revenue Calculator (FBA Revenue Calculator) and all you have to do is copy the ASIN from the product in the tool page and paste it into the calculator. Amazon will calculate these numbers through Net Profit and Net Margin and will also consider shipping fees—the normal FBA fees the product costs and the selling fees to hold the account with them. There are even coupon codes for these product listings that will give a foot-up on any purchases being made for new inventory to flip.

Become aware of the annual rates and the typical pricing of the products because if there needs to be a change of selling, the owner will already be steps ahead with their choices of products. Certain products are trending right now and if it is the best motive for the business to stay in a trending light, then we must use the tools mentioned to keep track of what products are going to be listed next. Sometimes, companies sell Online Arbitrage (OA) for trending profits and knowing that the company is going to see spikes in visitors and buyers alike, this will create a safe playing field for buyers that are coming from everywhere to get it from your shop. Unfortunately, these trends do not last forever so there cannot be a constant influx of revenue coming from these products, and that is why it is crucial to have product diversity.

Product Diversity

Having product diversity is something that cannot just be mastered if there is no prior research done. First, one of the many things that need to be done is to check around for available units and once that is done, we are going to do internal searches about the product knowledge of our investment. There may be a product that you can scoop up and list online exclusively to the point where only customers will come to your shop to buy. This is going to be an exclusive market but great for any startups that are trying to get enough sales to see their return on the quarter budget. Choose great products but in the end, if you want to make the most money in these quests, there needs to be a product choice that stands out and one that can be stood by for quite some time. A good product will stand in the inventory and move at a rate that leaves the company restocking the items in a timely manner that also adds up with their revenue charts.

This is why it is crucial to try a few products first before you begin buying in huge quantities that will sell half across the nation in full. These products need to stand above the others and be the better price to be able to flip for a great profit in one go or in multiple goes. Make do with some of the products that are in stock but do not just purchase as if these are the only products on the market, otherwise there is going to be losses taken for any budgeting that is spent incorrectly. To list those products on dropshipping sites is also going to cost a fee so we want to make sure that the products that we do list on the website are going to sell, and that they are not going to just take up space in our shop. If the products do not end up selling and they are taking up space inside of the shop shelves, then there will need to be more space purchased for more processing rates that are not required only because the shop has all of these products that are not being bought or shipped out. This is going to create problems for inventory flow because, at the point of the startup, there needs to be one hundred percent efficient use out of every penny of the spending budget. Look at the annual selling rates of these products and look at the SKU to specifically zero in on the product everyone is talking about right now. If you can get this product down to a T, then we will be able to move forward with mass inventory purchasing if the product really does sell. If it is a high-end product, then we can surely say we will know the quality of it once we track down all of the information and customer info about it.

Chapter 4: All Ways to Do Retail Arbitrage

There are many ways a company is going to be selling OA and we are going to talk about them in this chapter. The ways are going to consist of other online distributing markets that manage multi-channel fulfillments for all of its dropshipping users, and it connects the buyers to the sellers in order for everyone to make their sales and purchases. These systems will receive profits from the arbitrage that is being sold on these accounts and there will be fees associated with all of the products and package plans for selling with them. Utilize these systems when you need a secure form of buyers and when you want to let the customers come to you. With great reputations within the selling world, it is going to be an advantage to work with these companies because they will be able to assist startup companies and provide many tools that are necessary when running an online shop or commerce outlet. We are going to discuss one of the first ways to sell OA and the first one is going to be with Amazon.

Amazon

Selling OA on Amazon is getting increasingly easier every year and there are just a few simple steps that one will have to take before they begin making sales. With this route, you are going to be able to choose through 20 different product categories that are open to all sellers to choose a product to sell. The next step is going to be to calculate the number of units that you want to sell. Choose a plan with Amazon to be able to sell a fixed or unlimited number of products and pay a fee of $39.99 as a monthly subscription. If the company chooses an individual plan, they are going to pay a $0.99 fee for each one item sold and after the product is sold, the company will pay selling fees.

Develop an account on the Seller Central section of Amazon and begin registering your products to the web. List the products on the account that are going to be sold and add things to the catalog as individuals or as by bulks to the account. This is when the company has the opportunity to stick with the products that are already on Amazon and use these product descriptions given, which will include shipping options or conditions of the product. If they do not want to go with this opportunity, they will be able to list products that are not yet on Amazon and there can be a customized system made for the products imported with custom SKU and UPC/EAN codes.

eBay

With eBay, there is going to be an easy going approach to selling OA and the first thing that needs to be done is to sell your items on eBay. Confirm all of the account and seller details and add an automatic payment method for the eBay fees that will be charged using their services. Create a listing and upload photos of your listing right from a mobile device. The amount of money eBay charges the seller to list the product is going to depend on how much the item's price and category is. Performance on the seller is even a factor when they are charging the seller these fees. They will charge insertion fees for every item on the list and if the company decides to list an item in two separate categories, then they will additionally pay a second insertion fee for the second category. Every month, the company will get up to 50 insertion fees listings or more if you have an eBay store. Although, selling limits apply and certain categories for selling are excluded from the zero insertion fee rates and to get these zero insertion fees, one must reside in the United States and excluding other territories. There is a final value fee when an item is sold or if eBay determines that the sale was completed outside of eBay. The Final value fees are calculated through a percentage of the total amount the buyers pays including shipping and handling but not including sales tax.

Through eBay, there are two different types of listing formats and they can reach out to many different customers that are looking for different types of deals. First, there is auction-style listing and with this, the total amount of the sale is the auction start price, listed as well as the Buy It Now price, the Reserve pricing or the price identifiable between the buyer and seller, typically being the highest price. The other listing format is going to be by fixed pricing and this will be a normal sale across the board, which will include a fixed price that is determined by the seller and not the buyer.

Beware of not meeting the standards because if there is weak performance selling through eBay, there may be additional fees applied during the final value fee calculation. If the account does not meet the minimum seller performance standards in the United States, sellers will receive an additional

4 points percentage fee on the standard final value fee and this will make it harder to ramp up production. If you have ratings of the products that are 'Items Not as Described' and in the service metrics listed as **Very High,** your final value fees will also increase by 4 percentage points.

There are many ways to accept payment through the eBay systems and some of these include PayPal, credit or debit card, merchant cards, or payments on pickup. You can check all current statuses on payment through an internal link called the Seller Hub within eBay or My eBay. There is always good support for any payments pending or held up by some form of transactional occurrence.

Private Labeling

Private labeling is coming into the OA scene very strong with its diversity and personalization toward the crowds. Products are able to be labeled through different branding companies and the products are able to be sold at greater values for certain sources and communities that do not have other possible means of receiving other brands or great deals. Private labeling systems offer high-quality items with greatly reduced prices and it rubs off on the daily consumer by presenting them with great items that are not charged to a ridiculous value as they could be otherwise. Considering the brand name on the packaging is what makes the product cost so much, and customers everywhere are settling for white labeled products that give them the same quality and do not break the bank for any purchases that need to be made once or frequently. Consumers on average recommend or pay more for a brand that gives them the personalization for the service or product value that is given or purchased. This is because they value the personal product of their choice, and this leads to companies creating exclusive campaigns for their products when there are special events like roadshows to showcase the products. Private labeling companies are trying to compete with these big box companies that have plenty of distribution space so the rise of white labeling will stay steady until the labeling company makes a move to start manufacturing their own products for example. But the fact is that there are at times more value in these white labeling companies because they use a good product to back up their new name to the scene. Some companies develop really good names for themselves right at the beginning of their ventures, and this is going to be a strong backbone for any of the sales and clientele growth of the company.

Multi-Channel Fulfillment

Multi-Channel Fulfillment (MCF) gives a wide array of options and tools for the company that is getting ready to list their inventory up. Through MCF, the company will be allowed to engage with the Amazon customer, the personal website customer, extra dropshipping customers, and other online customers that come to purchase. This expands the selling horizons for customers everywhere to come and join in. Submit orders for the Amazon marketplace to fill and manage the customer service for all orders filled. Other advantages include being able to have returns sent back to you or back to the fulfillment center and returned to your online inventory. This is going to optimize when you want a product to be listed for sale on the account, and when there are going to be special items up for list for seasonal or special events coming up in the year. MCF is going to create a better and more specified selling route for the company, as they will be able to approach and market to the customer in different ways before they ultimately get the items in their shopping cart and check out.

Chapter 5: Researching and Choosing the Right Product

Requirements for deciding what products to buy and sell

Tap into all the markets that relate to your product and your product demographic. The greatest way to tap in is going to be by utilizing tools that are going to create lists of all of the products to choose from. The Tactical Arbitrage tool is only one of the many ways that the company will be able to track down info about the product and generate flow formulas of the expected revenue to be made. It is not always about choosing a pretty product over another, or one that has functional needs that compete with the other operating devices on the market. Deciding on the right product is going to take some time if the company is willing to put the research necessary to find out what is going to be the most fiscally responsible product to buy for redistribution. Does the product have a low ROI so that it can make typical sales while creating higher profit margins?

Consider the facts of the products and what the true numbers are going to make you in return. The product does not have to be the best product of our time because times change and we must be aware of these things. The product just needs to be strong on its own and it needs to have buyers that are looking for this product everywhere around the world. It can be a product that only some of the age verification can purchase and on the other hand, it can be a product that is sold exclusively to adults that are 21+ of age. The main factors that need to be considered are the cost of the product and the total costs of the seller fees when they decide to list on certain providing sites. When you begin to acquire trustworthy suppliers and creating a more unique product sale or product line for sale, there is going to be a solidified idea for sourcing. Trustworthy partners will establish good relations between selling in the e-commerce platforms if there is good rapport built early and further on into the services request. Good relationships with the suppliers are going to bring upon opportunities that can discount shipping fees or possible items from distributors. Even if these shipping fees are only a 1 or 2% rates influx, it can still benefit on larger order fulfillment through the companies. Ideas will be worked out for the indulgent of the companies and the benefit packages that suit the service requests.

Manufacturers and Distributors

Good knowledge when thinking of your suppliers is going to be that you have a few options to pick from when dealing arbitrage. The first option is going to likely be manufacturers, and purchasing this way typically involves independent contractors or representatives that partake in the labor and marketing of any number of companies. Typically with this case, the prices are usually lower because of the type of structure. Distributors that are also known as wholesalers or brokers buy in quantity from several manufacturing companies and store the goods in a common mass inventory for goods for sale to retailers. The warehouse full of inventory can price the products higher than that of the manufacturer and satisfy the needs of the common customer.

Importing

Importing goods from other countries or territories can be good but there can typically be a great freight cost for the goods. These are necessary steps to take when considering high-end goods that are not found in the states but are very popular in home-culture or in stores in other areas brought to attention through social media.

Freelance Brokers and Special Goods

There are some distributors that are independent and that also make special or custom items that are specific or nonspecific to the buyer or mission of the company. Items like these could also be high-end and they could have requirements or specified documentation of purchase or credit check. These items can be sold at roadshows or conventional expos and could be a local commodity as well.

Where and How to Find the Right Products

When looking for the right products to distribute, one must start questioning what is being purchased currently. There are products on the shelves ranging anywhere home goods to garden goods and industrial alike. There are many chains of companies that need to be supplied for the right price. We highly recommend using the tool that is called Tactical Arbitrage and finding ways to make a personalized search using the tool for all suppliers on the market. There are suppliers that you may not know about, as well as suppliers that may need to be found after hours and hours of scouring through lists and lists of products. This is okay if you find yourself not knowing who to go with at first because it is going to be an investment that defines your quarterly profit. This is a good chance to compare companies and the different qualities that all of them establish to the dropshipping crowds. Most of the time, the company is going to find out that working with a great distributor or manufacturer will really make a big difference for also selling a good product. Having a good experience with the service providers like this is going to open new gateways for other benefits within the company. You will never know what they will be like without purchasing a couple of different products first.

Trustworthy Suppliers

Trusting suppliers as they trust you is crucial and time sensitivity is also a great habit to upkeep if there is going to be a lot of shipments being sent out. Cooperation is a great habit for trust building. If there are red flags that go up about certain suppliers, it is not good to just wait around for things to get better. Some simple problems with these providers can be items running out of stock or failed shipment/wrong shipment sent to the customer. There can be delays on the products through the warehouse even though time stamps could have been made with arrival dates forwarded out. One of the main product failures to happen usually comes down to product inspection and if the buyer does not get the correct product or product quantity, there has to be refunds and reorders. There usually will be a quality control aspect here and possibly someone to even manage that position for the company.

Where to Buy the Right Items to Sell at High Margin

Wholesaling

We are going to talk about what a wholesale account is and how it is an example of how purchasing in high margin is profiting for e-commerce. Setting up a wholesale account with a company is easy and once the two companies are affiliated, then documents like the EIN are exchanged and the process goes from there. It can be done in minutes for most companies. Once the account is in place, there will be a whole catalog of products to choose from and this doesn't have to be just from one source as we mentioned before with the Tactical Arbitrage tool. Hundreds of wholesaling companies will be listed and this will be the opportunity to browse and compare items that are going to be purchased in bulk quantities. Consider not where the product is going to be found but more possibly where the product comes from, and the more middlemen in between you and the product is going to create more fees that take away from your profit.

Sourcing Products from a Cheap Market

There could be some huge advantages to ordering product from cheap vendors. One of the good things is that there will be a lower minimum order and it will overall be cheaper on the spending budget allowing room for more to purchase if wanted. There are going to be thousands of outlets to choose from here since they will always have these products, meaning that the company can start off small and build up. Most products like this come white labeled from cheap vendors and it creates a great source for decent quality for better prices in the markets. There are concerns with dealing with cheap markets and this could be false product marketing and untimely links that support the wrong listings. Some listings can be paid for but taken down right after if you are not in contact with the main person of the marketing or sales team. Get in contact with someone specifically when dealing with these types of markets to make the easiest time for constant arrival dates and payment stamping. Don't deal with markets that are so cheap that they do not have value, as well as markets that have great value but not communication. If the company does not communicate properly with the sales team, then there cannot be business conducted because of poor ethics. If there is ever a moment to accept payment at any time that is not part of the wholesaling purchase, then this is a red flag to look out for. The companies should always bring up shipping and freight costs so that the customer is always aware of how the costs of the products are going to lay out for the future. Get to know markets that are not pricey and see what markets you can find your product in if this is your market.

Find a supplier

Site 1: Alibaba

https://www.alibaba.com/

Alibaba distributes thousands of products across its site and they even have ties within AliExpress which have a presence across the whole globe. Companies can trade anything from glass products to industrial agents throughout the site. There are great prices and at large quantities for anyone in a dropshipping company looking for a new source.

Site 2: DHGate

https://www.dhgate.com

There are going to be plenty of products to choose from at DHGate and even though there are a lot of white-labeled products here, it is going to be a great place to go for anything that is quality. They have seasonal deals that range up to 90% off and they even have a coupon system that allows for further markdowns.

Site 3: AliExpress

https://www.aliexpress.com/

This site comes with a great variety of categories to choose from which can suit anyone's needs even if they are looking for only apparel. They have a coupon system and coins for benefits earned through using the service and making purchases.

Chapter 6: What is the FBA Process and How Does it Work?

What do you need before starting FBA?

Before starting with FBA selling, the company is going to need to get a couple of things in line. First off, the company will get accounts set up with any wholesaling companies and this can include establishing an EIN. Here are some simple steps to take when beginning FBA. First, gather all of the proper business information together which can include the address and contact information. Second, we are going to make a business email that can be associated with the accounts that we open up. Next, you are going to set up an international credit card for any orders that will need to be placed. Have a Business account Tax ID, as well as State Tax ID set up beforehand that you can document the business with. The next will fall into place once you get to the site store and open up a seller account. Open a seller account and pay the fees so that you can begin listing products for sale. List the products to sell and make a selling goal that will align with the current assets and get ready for your first sale.

Rules of the Amazon marketplace

The rules of FBA are quite simple and not too many to follow. As an FBA marketer, the company is going to need to learn the standards of what it takes to represent the products through Amazon and to create appropriate product listings. All products that are sold through Amazon are required to have a manufacturer barcode that goes along with the product to follow it through its shipping, and this is going to be complete with the FBA Labeling Service. Learn all the requirements for transporting the boxed and labeled goods to Amazon fulfillment centers. You will need to learn about the inventory storage limits that are given by Amazon to store inventory within the database. Create great product descriptions and content information to submit for the products that are being posted on.

The FBA System

The FBA system works for Amazon bringing in new distributors that are willing to represent the company. Companies source products from Amazon's distributors or otherwise some other third party, and they import the inventory directly to Amazon's database. The company then re-prices the products and puts them up for sale on Amazon. This creates affiliate marketing without having to be in a tight hold to the company and its policies. With this system, the company is going to decide how much it truly wants to sell as well as the products that are going to be sold. Through FBA, high volumes of customers are coming around when they see a name like Amazon and this is going to supply a consistent trust factor for all of the customers who may be new to the company selling the arbitrage. There are tools a company can use to track down the better deals on these distributing lists of products to choose from. These tools can find out where the product is being sourced from and the comparison of all of the products that are alike or in the same category. Pick a category that you will like to list your product in and address that this is going to be the go-to category for your product. Once you decided the category, the company is going to pay fees for the inventory space and the right to place the product online for sale. Calculate these costs using the FBA calculator to get a rough idea of what the company is going to be spending. Things to keep in mind are the complete entirety of the fees that Amazon is going to be charging. There are seller fees which are charged when each product is sold. There are labeling fees if there are no proper labels—Amazon will slap a charge on the packages for having to do your job for you. There are FBA Prep Service and FBA Unplanned Prep Service fees that will be addressed if the shipment goes out wrong and if there are improperly prepped products. Selling with Amazon is going to expand the reach across the globe and allow the company to double its reach by selling to countries everywhere. There are up to 180+ countries to distribute through Amazon's global reach with over 170 fulfillment centers that can be used to the company's shipping advantages. The FBA system is going to be a pioneering venture for anyone who is looking to expand their company past more than just a personal website. This system is going to allow two companies to represent each other and double profits through each shipment. Amazon has plenty of products they can choose from if sourcing is one of the harder parts for the company. If the company does not know what product to dedicate their time to, Amazon will help with purchasing different products until the right one is found to purchase bulk. Purchasing bulk isn't always necessary and good progress can be made with individual sales as well, but depending on the programs that are chosen, Amazon will determine the profits that the products are going to generate. A budget is crucial when selling with FBA because there are going to be fees that need to be paid for any product that will be going up for sale.

The Approach of the FBA System to Retail Arbitrage

Selling retail arbitrage through the FBA system is going to be a perfect match for the company. Marking down the items to put back up in the inventory is going to create a safety net for the profits that are going to come in. The fees for Amazon FBA are going to take away somewhat from the sales if the price points are not right. The fees by Amazon FBA are going to need to accumulate to a breakeven price for the profits that the products are sold for. Create a great formula that is going to bring in marginal profits even if they are not huge differences. Amazon knows that there are markets that need to be filled and there are products right now that can distribute for the trending quarters. Amazon is more than willing to share the limelight and make commission together once a company decides that they are going to source their products through Amazon. If a company has trouble getting their products to their customers, Amazon is going to help with their shipping and handling programs. Amazon will take responsibility for the shipping of the products if you can find a way to properly box and write descriptions for the products that are being moved. Instead of putting all of the money into a distribution center that holds all inventories, Amazon is going to hold the products through their fulfillment centers and these centers will be able to store and ship the products that the company owns. This frees up a lot of responsibility from the company owner since they do not need to pay for their own warehouse fees and taxes. Not having a warehouse is going to create a lot of freedom for the business owner to make other moves in the shop. Utilizing Amazon FBA is a great way to make residual income if the company is not making big moves like purchasing in bulk. If the company only has a few items to list, then this could be a great way to earn trust through Amazon for customers to make great experiences buying our products. A great advantage that Amazon is going to give to the company that is sourcing through Amazon is by customer service. Any customers that purchase the OA through Amazon is going to need a proper customer service center. Thankfully, Amazon has one of the best customer service centers online and this can accomplish many things. If there are customers that are concerned and may not have received their products yet, Amazon will be able to assist in getting all of the information organized and present solutions for the customers. This can become an important tool to take advantage of if the company does not already have a customer resolution center to help others. Keeping up with customers across the globe is going to be hard, especially considering the fact that some will be in different time zones and some will have time-sensitive schedules that are going to affect when the products are received and used. Instead of the company only being run by one or a few employees, which that would be with a typical dropshipping site, Amazon is going to step in and be a leading guide for the companies flipping their profits. OA is going to generate revenue by leading competing price wars with each product of choice. These products are set at a certain margin to obtain profits for the sellers, but there has to be a proper formula that is going to make a perfect sale every time to turn those gains into profits. After the shop is stocked a few times over, the company is going to begin accumulating more and more inventory that is not being sold. With this new inventory, new prices can be set and these products can be sold to make new profits as long as it aligns with the formula created. Remember that these products cannot be sold for free because Amazon will even charge for the seller's fee when the product leaves for shipment.

Chapter 7: How to Sell Products with the FBA System

Starting with Amazon FBA

Once the FBA system is set up, we can move onto selling the products. Create an account and logging into the Seller Central, you can proceed to "Add a Product" in the drop-down menu. There are many ways that the business allows products to be listed. First, you can add products that are already products of Amazon. You can create a new product listing which can include exporting goods for redistribution. The other option is to upload multiple products at once and this will be good for uploading bulks that do not have specific qualification for posting. Now that the product is created in the system, you can now designate this product to a specific category within Amazon and that will be by choosing features or browsing actual categories. Mind you, that the products that you choose to list have listing fees and this will include if the company lists an individual product in two separate categories. The product listing is going to be broken down into several information factors and this will be the chance to list any information about it that will be helpful to the consumers. These lists are going to include "Vital Info, Keywords, Images, Description, Variations, Offer, and More Details." There is an option to only use FBA for certain shipments or for certain products so you will need to go through the account and manually decide what products are going to be shipped through Amazon FBA. If you are selling new items that are not on Amazon, you will be able to use sticker less, commingled inventory. If someone orders from you and there is a more convenient placement, Amazon will source this item from a warehouse possibly closer and this will allow the company good shipping times for the customer since there are many fulfillment centers that can fulfill state by state.

Shipping and Handling with FBA

Once you begin listing more products on your database, Amazon is going to ask you to create a shipping plan and your packing type. There are two packing types in FBA which include "Individual Products" and "Case-Packed Products". Case-Packed Products are going to be sets or packs of the products that are better sold unseparated. When the shipping plan is created, you can add all of the items to the list for sale. You can keep adding extra items and they will populate in the database, but since you have already created a new shipping plan with the address, you can now select "Add to an Existing Shipping Plan." When you are getting ready to finally ship the products to Amazon, make sure to clarify whether the products are going to be labeled by Amazon or not. The time is going to come when the packages need to be weighed before being sent off to Amazon fulfillment centers. After weighing all of the packages, you can then print out all of the labels to stick onto packages for mailing as soon as you're ready. Check all packages and drop them off at the local UPS store for sending off. Some sellers are allowed to set their own shipping rates they can charge the Amazon customers.

Setting up your Amazon Seller Account

You will have to decide what type of seller you are going to be and the options are professional seller or individual seller. Professionals are usually sellers with a plan to list more than a few handfuls and with a goal to remain a regular seller in the company progress. Individual sellers usually have smaller amounts of products that are trying to sell for something that of residual income and someone that may not be able to keep up with ordering bulk products.

List Your Product

To begin listings your product, there must be a budget system in play for all of the fees that will need to be paid to Amazon. There is a monthly fee for all professional sellers and they are charged $39.99 monthly fee for the accounts to be active in FBA. Individual sellers may not have to pay this fee, but this still will have to pay a selling fee every time. Individuals are charged $0.99 for every item that is sold. Professional sellers do not have this listing fee and this is great to take advantage of when buying bulk. If the company is planning on selling more than 50 units of product each month, then it will be beneficial to pay the $39.99 monthly fee considering that each sale is going to cost before there is a breakeven around $40. Amazon is also going to charge a referral fee on the combined price of the product and the shipping costs so choose the right price to maximize with the most profits.

Choose the Right Price

Choosing the right price is going to be crucial for gaining customer retention. The company is going to have to choose a price that is going to be right with the distributors and is going to be well-beneficial for the customers. Most likely, the customer is going to come first and there needs to be a clearly defined product worth that is going to rub onto the consumer as well. This needs to be a universal price that lines up with other products that are similar to yours but in different ranges of quality and other factors. You are going to want to design a price that stands out from the other products next to yours, but also one that keeps it inside of the field of value. You may not want to go any cheaper than the other companies that may be doing business with you and this will be better not to, considering you have fees to pay for the services used. Keep the price simple and keep moving inventory in and out to create a consistent selling system. If you can successfully source and sell these products at a formulated rate, you will be able to ramp up production by purchasing more and more inventory or site-space for the inventory. Once you begin to ramp up production for the company, there are going to be extra assets added and one of them should definitely be extra inventory. With the extra inventory, accumulating this is going to give the opportunity to make extra sales and to create special events with great offers on the items. This is going to be great marketing if the company decides to sell the OA on Amazon and migrate all extra viewers to the personal website to market for other reasons. Other than marketing, it is also going to bring in more sales that are dedicated to the website alone and no other service providers. This is going to maximize all profit potential since the website doesn't need to pay listing or selling fees to anyone.

Care Plan for Reimbursement or Refunds

There are a few ways you are going to get your refund through Amazon FBA if there is any miscalculation for the services provided. If the items are destroyed without your request or permission, orders for which the weight fee or dimensional fee has been overcharged. Even if a replacement product was sent to the customer but the original has not been sent back to the company, there will be a refund. If there is a refund that needs to be issued, you can start the case by doing it yourself or hiring a virtual assistant to document the changes and information. If you do it yourself, prepare to cross-reference sales reports through Amazon that can take up time and effort. The best part about it is that you will not be paying anyone to track your actions and the downside will be that the owner will need to be prepared for these steps. It can be time-consuming and a lot to handle if someone has never tried to do it before.

Hiring a virtual assistant has its ups and its downs when it comes to solving refunds. The assistant will practically do most of the job for you, and they will be able to cross-reference the sales data and even make claims through the Seller Central. Even though the assistant will be helpful, they will still need some guidance in getting all of the information for the company completely right. They will have to understand how the FBA mistakes are made and what courses to take once the right information is gathered. One of the downsides of this strategy is that you need to pay for their services so let's just hope that refunded package is worth it.

Make Your First FBA Shipment

The first step you are going to take in Seller Central is going to be to find the "Manage Inventory" button. Mark the item that you are interested in using and click "Send/Replenish Inventory." On the ShipBob Dashboard, select "Inventory

Transfer" and then transfer the inventory to the desired location. Each FBA shipment needs to be entered as a unique transfer. This shipping ID is going to be located for further documentation on the Seller Central dashboard. Reserving the inventory date is going to be the process where the distributor is going to pick your order. The 'Ship Date" will be picked out and that will be the date that the product is sent out to the consumer. Once the draft order is created, you can then decide which items you want to send and this needs to line up with whatever you documented for the FBA shipment. You are then going to upload sticker PDF for each of the items added within the Seller Central. Create updates for the shipment through FBA and download the box and shipping labels while the weight and dimensions of the order will be the next steps. Just an extra note for shipping is included. For freight, Amazon FBA orders will have a fifteen hundred pound weight limit per pallet. For parcels, Amazon FBA orders will have a fifty-pound weight limit per box. Attach the box labels and get the package ready for shipping. In the database, the transferred inventory will remain in transit until it arrives at the Amazon fulfillment center. When the product arrives, confirm its arrival, then you are going to the Seller Central and confirm, along with a new balance of your inventory.

Manage the Whole Business of Retail Arbitrage with Amazon FBA

It is possible to manage the whole business flow straight from Amazon FBA. There are system templates that can be utilized to create an easy-going work atmosphere. Every step of the FBA system can be scaled through any means of production and it doesn't need to be a company moving thousands of units at once. FBA can be used by sellers alike all over the world, even if they are selling custom goods that are individual units by one-time sales. These types of practices can make a high-price item stand above all of the rest once buyers realize they are going to get it for a better value, or when they will receive expedited shipping when they purchase through your company. Giving customers incentives to buy is going to be a great skill to administer, but once things get rolling nicely, there should be buyers coming in without the need of a special event of a discount sale. Amazon FBA is going to come along with Amazon's great customer support center and this is going to be a great advantage to be taken when there are customers that need assistance with their shipments. For possible purchases, Amazon is going to link the buyer and the seller by letting them communicate any problems or product questions that cannot be answered. You can manage the whole thing with the right work ethics and some companies will even go as far as to say there will be a loss of control somewhere down the line. This is not going to be an actual loss of control, but rather a sophisticated step into becoming more of a manager than just a contributor. There will still be a great aspect of control and all that will come about is going to be the adjustment of responsibilities since these systems are going to be handling the rest.

Chapter 8: Scaling Up Your FBA Business

Scaling up the Amazon FBA business is not going to be a quick feat. This is not typically the case for businesses that are only making penny profits. There may have to be some product purchasing that gives the company an extra boost for quarterly profits. Usually, the company is going to pick from one to a few products to sell on the site. Purchase a great product that is going to be a money maker for the next coming quarters so that you can begin thinking of the next step. Once there has been enough revenue generation from the product that has been showing promising sales, keep flipping this product until there is a sum of money that is for investing further into the company. Use these gained profits to purchase more of the same product especially at a lower rate if you are purchasing into the next capacity brackets. If you do not want to purchase the same product, use some of the profits to purchase another product and list it to create a greater revenue flow. Now, products that sell are going to be helping each other keep a consistent profit rate.

Once you begin scaling up within Amazon FBA, there are going to be greater benefits with the service providers that are chosen to deal with these shipping deals. Amazon will give percentage points back on money spent on products that Amazon is listing and when the company sells these items, they will get them for a better price when they purchase in bulk. Once the company begins to ramp up, it will be good to optimize the products that are on the market. You can categorize the product differently, or place product ads to make an extended reach to certain buying crowds. Change up the product descriptions a bit to be more poppy for the consumer and watch the variations you make because some of them will bring in more buying traffic all because it is merely being optimized. A brand new look to the site can do some justice if things have been years before seeing a changeup, so don't be afraid to make new changes to the company that can promote new viewers to come. You can scale up the business by changing up the budget balance, and where most of the money made may have been going back into the inventory, we can think about new changes that can make a great difference to the flow. You are owning success in one category on Amazon, but how about creating two different product listings that can account for two different categories which can practically double the profits for the company. These are also going to be new learning curves for the company if they are diving into territory that has not been touched before. Finding great products to resell isn't always the easiest, but once you get the hang of it, you are going to have a hand in a few markets by the time you know it. Product choice is going to evolve as the company gets more exposure and as customers may begin to ask about different product variations, whether it be about other colors or other sizes and makes.

Methods for Obtaining Reviews

Create methods to obtain feedback from the fans and supporters of the e-commerce shop. There are tons of ways to get feedback from great individuals sharing their opinions about the product. Good and bad products alike will end up getting sometimes the truest opinions of the lot. Terrible products make consumers rant and give bad reviews for products, but these are often at times publicity stunts to gain some other type of revenue. Very good quality products are going to have the buyers rave about the purchase online, and this could be by having comments left on the page or by custom pictures being taken and left for others to see, and also judge the product by other visual enhancements. Pictures of the products on social media sites can also obtain reviews just by visual enhancement marketing tactics. Run a page that has your content on it and you will obtain followers. Invest time in a good marketing foundation that could be a separate firm running strong with the company, and they will handle all inbound traffic and possible leads. Reviews are great for those in the community that does not own the product yet. Now, think locally just on your site that means creating a comfortable atmosphere so that the consumers rate your shop good on the e-commerce platforms you decide to sell through.

Move into Wholesale

Merchants typically sell goods that are not purchased or selected in advance and before the products are sent to the consumers. Good products will bring sales and the customer orders leaving the consumer to price the product as they please. They purchase it at a wholesale value so it can have a high margin as long as you can still balance out a low ROI. Begin making connections with wholesaling companies that have products that are in your field. Pick a good product and the consumer will enjoy the variety when you present them with different costs for different qualities. It is going to be a ramp-up in price so mind that this step is going to require a bigger budget. Save up for this step so that you can purchase your first hundred units or five hundred units. These are stepping stones that are going to teach us the basics of OA. Good suppliers will give great prices when purchasing these quantities and when it gets into the thousands, it can really get to discount season. This is going to lead to a high yield for the consumer to place these new gains aside to save for their new steps. Let the product sell itself if you know it will. When visiting these wholesalers, look at how much they have shipped out before. Ask about their markets and who is typically buying or whatever curiosity you have and get to know your wholesaler.

Move into Private Labeling

Your Own Product

Some companies build revenue to brand their own products and this could be great for the overall marketing of the company. Labeling companies are doing business with thousands of sources right now that have an amazing number of products to choose from. Labeling companies work with any type of labeling designs or artistically enthused branding. When the company starts branding its own product, they will be able to have a customized product that is unlike any other. This product will be able to stand out and they will be able to design it to have a label or a box that shines. Generally, the white-labeled products aren't going to be the most original looking types of things because they are made in mass quantities. So it is necessary to go to external sources for possible artwork handling or logo designing that needs to be taken care of before this phase. Get creative with this step because there are going to be tons of competitors that are using the same methods as you. For all you know in the world of white labeling, the competitors could be using the same company as you for these services. Use this chance to create an unforgetful image for the customer to remember the product by. These private labeled companies are going to make it easy for consumers to diversify the product every quarter. Make ways to keep the product looking interesting even if it means doing some boxing as well the same ways and make it clever and efficient to receive your packages.

Other's Products

When purchasing white-labeled products that are from other sources, the best part about that is going to be the price. There are great prices for locally made things that can be considered common goods and these goods can be purchased as well as wholesale and they can be flipped through OA. Avoid shipping costs to outlets and purchase locally to pick up with a truck or van. With these products, most customers do not know what the product actually is because it tends to be a plain form of a product that they are used to. These products may look like something they may know, but they could have no labels at all and just be a standalone product. This is okay if the product is high-quality, but the customer also relies on visual enhancements as we have spoken about in this book. Sell other products that are white-labeled to exclusive buyers and give good deals so that these buyers come back on a frequent basis. These products are best for buyers who are only looking for quantity and quality is typically the second concern. There are a lot of white-labeled great products out there and the quality just keeps getting better and better as the years of online shopping go on.

Advertise the Products

Marketing Firms

Marketing firms are a great way to get a product or a distributor a proper representation. Marketing firms are masters of the market and they can tap into most streams of public interest. These markets do anything from making phone calls to independent advertising that could be state to state by roadshows or other means of trade traveling. These firms hire good representatives that are well-established in their skills to be able to make online advertisements or ones of that in the retailer or at community areas as spokespeople. These opportunities usually come by advancements into the business markets all around. There can be special events made where companies make appearances by sponsorship and furthermore, these firms are going to be the perfect ones to go for to get it all organized. Marketing firms also generate other high forms of online traffic with their own servers, and this, in turn, is going to give you boosts to your traffic in buyers. A great team of marketers will charge for their services but it is quality effort to make sure that the company is being run to a certain degree of standards which can be designed to the company's needs. Marketing agencies create and establish a strategy which overall can conduct market survey research, and they can also build great relationships with your audience and increase exposure to the company, by engaging with potential customers that may be interested with the product you sell.

Telemarketing companies have a great hand in the marketing world. Companies like these have employees that make outbound phone calls to engage with future prospects and to take orders of any current. This is a vital role for any company that is handling a large quantity of shipments, considering that there is also a need for a customer service helpline established as well.

There are going to be digital marketing agencies that help improve the website, by advising to post or place social media accounts certain ways to market best to the viewers. Digital marketing can engage millions of customers around the world because they most likely are already on their device. Marketing firms tap in at the right time and also do extra promotions through the holiday times when it gets busier to keep up with the higher demand of traffic volumes.

Google Adwords

This tool is going to be vital if you are also using something like Google Ads. Google Adwords is a tool that acts a lot like a thesaurus which is a keyword identifier. Enter in the phrase you think your prospects are searching for in their browsers and Google will tell you similar phrases that may or may not relate. Google will tell the consumer how much a phrase is searched and how popular it will come to be in the end by the time someone buys it up. It is going to be costly for each keyword that is found, but it will really make the campaign boom if done properly with this tool. Use this tool if the company has not been named yet as a way to optimize the amount of traffic that can be earned through a different name.

Pay for Premium Accounts that Host Websites for Advertising

Paying for premium accounts is going to be a step when the company has had its time to adapt to the marketing world. This step is going to take more of the budget and it will be used to optimize more aspects of the online marketing tactics. Some of the optimizations that come with these platforms are unlimited bandwidth, unlimited domains, many different hosting partners like MSSQL and MySQL, more ram space can be purchased, and to even name the servers can be an option. Premium accounts are great for making the most out of the e-commerce platforms that are going to help market the inventory.

Improve the Quality of Your Listings

Make listings personalized through ways of Google Adwords. This is going to be a critical step in making great marketing moves. By optimizing Google Adwords to help decide on some of the most popular terms and phrases, while this is happening, the company is going to be placing ads about the products that are up for sale. These products are going to have great bios and strong reviews from past purchasers to ensure the new buyers will become interested in what they are looking into. By improving the quality of the listings this way with a clear decision to make ads that relate to the consumer, there will be a greater community reach for the company's market. Expanding the company's market is going to make room for more marketing tactics to be taken and more ads to be put up. There are so many social media platforms to put ads up on, and it is best to take advantage of them. It could be with companies like Facebook through Facebook Marketplace, or it could be with other companies like Shopify that help automate the ways a crowd will see the products even without a shop. Listings everywhere are going to be right alongside the listings that you have, and we need to make sure that our listings are going to be the ones that shine through others.

It does take good traffic to know what a quality listing looks like sometimes. With certain strategies, the right crowds can be brought in to buy, and these types of behaviors will as well make other buyers come to visit. But the company needs to know what it is going to take to bring high volumes of buyers to the site to keep the sales consistent. Otherwise, the company is going to be just searching for their crowds and they could be for years if they don't hone in on the ones who are truly going to benefit from their products. Finding a great audience isn't always going to be like finding a needle in a haystack, but it needs to be known that there are going to be a lot of varieties of customers that will also include one-time buyers. This is not going to be good for the company to rely on, especially if they are specializing in wholesaling products to other individuals. There needs to be a consistent stream of revenue, as well as a trustworthy group of buyers, that are going to be committed and connected to the company.

Creating great value on the ads that are placed is one of the first places we can start to achieve this success. These ads are going to speak to the audience in ways that make them relate to one another and appreciate the value of the product that you are supplying. This value has to shine above other products that are in the market that the customer is going to be aware of. These ads are going to remind them of the product quality and that there is an idea of urgency for the customer to come and get theirs today. When the ads are all set, it is time to fully customize the listings for the products to fit the true esteem of the customer. The customer is going to be able to relate to the product and its parts as long as there is a good time spent on the biography of the products and the endorsements laid out for the products. When creating better listings, we need to add more than just a couple of words and a review here and there. With a great listing comes personalization that speaks to the customer to let them know that their concerns are to be answered and figured out before they even have to put the item in the shopping cart. The product should have all of the knowledge necessary and it should have details that are special for the customer to know about that will possibly increase their chances of purchasing the products. The more effort you put into these bios, the more you are going to connect with the customer and their needs. All of their needs are going to be addressed, but they won't be if they don't read something that they need on the list. This is why it is good to put one hundred percent effort into making the best product descriptions for those that have not seen your products yet. Quality listings can become expensive if you are planning on just relying on paying a marketing firm to handle the work for you. They will make third-party listings of your product and they will do it on shopping forums or bulletins that are of the same degree or topic, and this is going to drive you great exposure to the company. Just mind that this is going to be a costly tactic as their services will be charging by the month. The firms are going to have so many outlets that are going to drive you more buyers, but once the fees stopped being paid, you will have no exposure and this is why it is good to have something to fall back on.

Great listings are going to receive higher ratings on optimizing sites with tools like Google Adwords. Great listings gain popularity by having interactions added to their queues. Some of these interactions can be by clicking buttons on the company site, or even minutes to seconds spent on certain pages of the site that will tell a lot to the company. Great listings are going to get better results for you to read the progress of the company selling points. You will be able to see if the customer stopped on a certain tab or on a certain product, and how long they took looking at the product or possibly reading their stats. These listings are going to gain popularity and begin to show at some of the top posts and topics of Google. People will be able to know about your company eventually if they search parts of your name and are clicking around to check for what they need online. Use these listings to keep at the top of the company website or on the FBA shipping lists so that you can make the best progress with your best-performing parts. There are going to be parts that work out really well for each other and that's going to make a great listing in itself. There just needs to be structuring for what product is going to be put up to the public, and which products are going to be left for the public to find by searching. If there is one thing for certain, there can never be enough ads done on a company as long as they are ready for the exposure. Never feel like you are going for too much ad space or relying too much on the advertisements that you do set out. These are going to build the company stronger every day the ad is up because your listing is going to shine above most others. There are going to be a genuine trustworthy aspect to note when these listings are being personalized for the customers. People are going to know that the company does not hide anything about their products and that they are honest with each and every customer putting into full consideration how the customer is going to be affected at the end of the day.

Use the Multi-Channel Fulfillment System

The next thing we are going to talk about in this chapter is about what Amazon's Multi-Channel Fulfillment is and how it is going to be practical to the selling world. Fulfillment by Amazon is only the beginning before it comes to Amazon's Multi-Channel Fulfillment (MCF) service and we can recap what FBA could accomplish for the company. The company taking their next step into working with a fulfillment center will result in greater efficiency when it comes to shipping, lowering costs, and your ability to deliver a better quality interaction for the consumer around the world.

FBA will allow access to smaller companies that can ship inventory to one of Amazon's 140 and more warehouse locations in the U.S. to be stored in a mass inventory until an order comes in. The company will then pick the product of their choice, process packaging, and ship the item to the customer. These transactions come with rates, but at the right selling capacity, things could really make a positive trend upward for sales.

MCF is a part of FBA and includes the same services but integrates with other platforms being sold on. Amazon will still store, pick, pack, and ship your inventory and these services are located all around the world, which includes countries like Canada, Germany, France, Italy, and Japan. Amazon's MCF may be a good option if you're selling on multiple e-commerce platforms already for the following reasons:

- You can spend more time tending to other aspects of your business, such as marketing, product sourcing, growing and defining your brand, and other activities that translate into more sales.

- Amazon's one and two-day shipping options could increase customer satisfaction and retention.
- Business opportunities won't be limiting the storage space problems for your inventory or warehousing fees.
- You can save time and money with fewer trips to the warehouse by leaving it to another warehouse to handle.

If you use FBA, your existing stock will serve customers on both Amazon and other sales channels. This makes it so MCF is available with or without FBA, and if you have a professional selling account, then you can list your MCF inventory without making it available for sale on Amazon. In addition to a $39.99 monthly subscription, MCF merchants are charged fulfillment fees for orders placed on their own website or other marketplaces, and that will mean that referral fees will not apply since the products weren't sold on its platform, which in this case is Amazon. We are going to list factors to consider when thinking of integrating MCF with FBA:

Great Customer Service

Amazon handles the physical process of the shipping means for you, and while FBA takes care of the merchant's customer service needs, MCF does not have a hand in this. Sellers are expected to update their customers with tracking and shipment information, as well as address any questions or concerns. This is going to be a huge task for the average company that is sending out 50 invoices a week. Having a great customer service roll in line is crucial for customer satisfaction to be one hundred percent. Every order can go with some form of interaction between the buyer and the seller, and it needs to be a role that is put into place early that can reflect the company's leading skills. This kind of behavior is going to encourage the buyers to come back feeling safe if it is the first time they are coming to the shop. Good customer service speaks volumes to the ones that are shopping on the site but have not made purchases yet. Offer a support tool for any buyers on the site that need a place to go to if they have any questions before purchase. Most times, the customer is going to have a question about the product either right before they purchase or right after they get their product, so having a good system in place for this is necessary. You want to make it the easiest as it possibly could be for the customer to have a good experience with the customer service your company gives. Never leave your customer with a sour feeling as they empty their shopping cart and close out of the shop because this can be easily avoided just by reaching out. Not every customer is going to love the shop, but as the company, it is an important role to lead when you want the customer to leave the site with a good feeling. Not pressuring the customer to purchase and not having reservations that can deter the customer away from spending valuable time on the site before their purchase. This is important for all companies to realize that their customers are the center of the mission and they should always come first. Given that Amazon has stringent rules considering customer service, it's worth investing in third-party software to ensure your performance metrics are up to speed with the site and all customer communication. When juggling several channels through these providers, you will need to keep tabs on the response times of each team member. This will decrease the chance of buyers leaving negative feedback. Negative feedback can follow the company for years if it's the right kind, and this is why it is important to have quality assurance for the customers that visit these sites. Even if there is negative feedback, the positive is always going to outweigh it and with constant product ads, it is going to make it an easy plot to keep the customers happy and engaged.

Whether you're using MCF or fulfilling these shipments yourself, Amazon FBA tracks each seller's response time to every one of their buyers. Merchants are expected to respond to customers within a 24-hour period after the message has been received through their Buyer-Seller Messaging system. This system is put in place to keep consistent communication between the buyers and sellers, and any problem or question that needs to be addressed. Keeping good track of response time is going to boost the rapport of the buyer to the seller that much more. It is going to be an important aspect of the sale to keep constant contact with the buyer through any discussions or onsite questions. The 24-hour window is going to be a good way to keep customer's trust as they know we are going to keep them on the top of the list of priorities. It can even be a better goal to set personal parameters that can amount to a 12-hour time window that can be a good cushion for any late responses that happen to turn up in the outbox. Use this cushion to stay ahead in any shipping communications that need to be arranged for the customer. Sometimes, customers are going to have specific shipping instructions and they are going to need to walk through the process with someone who knows what they are talking about, and this is going to be the perfect opportunity to take charge of their satisfaction. There are going to be customers that do not abide by this time window themselves, and you are going to reach out to the customers if there is no resolution. If there are returns pending, it is going to be hard to get the product back from the customer or even the return shipping label to them if they are non-communicative. This is why it is important to establish a trust bond early on into the relationship, which marketing firms can do very well. This bond is going to make the services and products fully transparent to the customer that is engaging. Take charge of all of the customer interactions that are going to take place on your watch because these faithful customers are going to remember every interaction that you set out in this company. Instead of having automated everything, which would make it automated customer service, it will be a healthy habit to add some humanity to it. There are going to be a lot of average people out there that are just trying to get products on their off days and there are going to be customers that need their products to them by the beginning of the week every week. We need to know how to handle these customers and how we are going to optimize their time to have them completely satisfied with the requests we fulfill. The quality of service your customers receive directly reflects their impression of your brand. This is going to be a great way to give your customer a great impression by the ways we treat them and their concerns. The brand will be able to gain awareness in the community just by doing right by all of the customers that choose to trust the company.

Consider a Shipping Location

It's a good practice to get an idea of which products make more sense for you to ship yourself instead of using Amazon's MCF service. Each item's weight, size, and measurement should be factored in before deciding if it makes sense to outsource fulfillment.

This is going to save time on the packing process as well and if you are paying fees for individual shipping slips, this will lower the cost by having the fulfillment centers print these labels with you.

To make fulfillment time and cost efficient, you are going to want to ensure the address you're shipping to is closer to Amazon's fulfillment center as opposed to the location where you'd be shipping the product out of yourself. This is going to loosen the constraints of having to live far from the shipping location. If the cost of shipping with Amazon's MCF exceeds the fees to take care of shipping in-house, then factor in what it will cost for 5 more shipments and save yourself the hassle by just paying less.

Order Personalization

Processing multiple orders quickly can mean it's harder to catch the details that may not be all correct for each process. Letting the small screwups will make all the difference in whether or not a customer returns a product or even returns to the store to buy ever again.

These are the information you'll need to enter for each order:

1. On the "Manage Inventory" page, select the items to be fulfilled.
2. In the drop-down menu on the same page, select "Create Fulfillment Order."
3. On the next page, enter the customer's details in the "Ship-to Address" field.
4. In the "Set Order ID" field, enter the order ID number.
5. Under "Print on Packing Slip," enter a new ID number (optional), as well as the order date and any additional comments you would like to send the customer.
6. Next, choose the desired fulfillment action and shipping speed.

7. The final step is to review your order before submitting it for final processing.

Once you submit an order to Amazon, the destination address cannot be changed so that is the time to double check all of the information. You will still have a 15-minute window of time in which you can cancel an order, though there is no guarantee it will be successful because the final process has already undergone. If there needs to be immediate cancellation, it would be best to contact a support agent that is suited to handle that type of case and open up a case ID with them so that they can assist you with the next steps.

Special Messaging

Amazon has the same standard of visual aesthetics in regards to shipping all merchant products. This means you're slightly limited when it comes to personal branding and customization. That being said, it's extremely important that you do everything in your efforts to add a personal touch to each shipment. This is going to make the customers find out that the company is going to go that extra mile to showcase the value of not only the product but the spirit of the shop too. Specialized boxing can be done with third party teams and these boxes or containers can be created to fit the customer's mindset or opinion set. There can be personal notes that are made for each customer or boxes that come in different variations to attract the visual aspects the customer will be enjoying. This is a good tactic for customers who enjoy buying products that stand out from the rest but have better missions that could involve charities or funds.

MCF doesn't offer a lot of options for the consumers as they prepare shipments. The Centers can either ship products in a plain brown box or in an Amazon-branded one. It can be okay to go with the typical branded box, but we have to consider personalization of the product for the customer and how the product is going to stand out from the rest. Regular boxes are going to be familiar to the customer and with Amazon's name on it, there is no doubt they won't light up when they see this name attached to their shipment. This can be a great marketing tool to rely on to allow the rapport of the company relationships to speak for the packaging experience. Amazon's name can be a great aspect for the company to wear with pride once their products are being shipped in their boxes. Before major profits are made and before the company is able to purchase customized boxing for the products, it will be cost efficient to utilize the boxes that Amazon will supply. Mind you, there will be set dimensions for these types of Amazon boxes but they will be good to use if the company is starting out by selling common goods that are of the same dimensions of the given Amazon boxes.

It could begin to become a bit confusing to your customers who have ordered products through non-Amazon channels. In this type of instance, receiving an Amazon-branded box when they ordered from your website may be frustrating and not what the customer would prefer. This is going to mix the customer up and it is going to leave them feeling like they do not know who they purchased from. There could be a product detail when listed that the company is going to be sent through multiple channels, or that it is going to arrive in a different box that has another company name on it.

It's best to make your decisions with goals of enhancing the customer experience rather than what seems convenient to you. There are going to be ways that will make the process the most convenient for you and with that, we are sure every product order can be a breeze. We need to also consider the need of the customer and remember that we must always put them first if we want to realize the part that they play for this e-commerce shop. Why not choose a customized packing slip that will have a special message from you to read to the customer? Things like this are going to drive the customer to happiness and they are going to come back to get that same feeling again. Completely optimize your customer's experience and get them to feel welcomed by making these systems relate to the customer.

Even though at the beginning of starting up your great sales, it's important to choose to send a special message to each and every customer regardless of what they've purchased. If it is a confirmation email with the customer's name in the subject line, great, we have nailed it, but it needs to be some type of personalized message that really leaves a customer feeling like you care. Design systems like this early on by creating a mail subscription list where you can send out personalized coupons or codes for redemption with the name of the customer on them that will make them feel special towards the shop. The customer is equally part of the family that makes up the product's mission and we must not forget to acknowledge all of the great the customer does by browsing through the shop and checking out everything that is up. Create personalized messages for the companies that you wholesale with, for example, in the holidays seasons when you want them to know you are thinking of their business during the times that matter the most. Design personalized invoices for the companies that you deal with so that they can feel like they are part of something that is a team effort. Once they feel more integrated with the company, they are going to want to spend more time and energy on the company that treats them like they are part of a bigger family. These messages can contain helpful words or just a simple thank you for shopping with their name attached. Even when there is communication with the customer, it is going to be within the best practice to refer to the customer by their names unless directed otherwise and to say special messages that can bond the customer to the seller. If the customer needs the company to give support, they should be treated with the most care and attention that can make them feel single importance that separates them from all of the other buyers. The customer needs to feel like you are giving them your full one hundred percent attention to their concern or act and that you are going to be right alongside to assist with the products. Create messages from one company to another that is set on the values of both companies. With this method, you can directly relate to the other customers by anchoring trust and common grounds. This is going to be great for the beginning of company relationships or the revamping of relations that are coming back to restock on the new inventory that just got to the shop. Messaging the customers is going to be a great habit to gain early communication from the customer in any case that they have anything that they want to review or bring up as a question. Customers are going to feel more welcomed to reach out for further concern if there is an initiative taken on the company's end to acknowledge the customer. Some customers are going to be a novice at the online purchasing processes, and they are going to need easy user-friendly website systems that can allow the whole buying parts to be easy to do.

Reminders

Amazon's Multi-Channel Fulfillment service is a great system to integrate for a way to grow your business on multiple sales platforms while accomplishing shipments and meeting your customers' delivery expectations. Fast shipping can work wonders for your reputation, but don't rely on just that because it also takes great customer service to make an organized pattern. It's important to stay on top of your support encounters even more so as you expand to more sales channels. The more sales the company is going to make, there can be a definite estimated increase in customer assistance orders that will come through. With having different products being sold, there need to be more variations to be able to describe the qualities of these goods and make better listings for the shop's presence. Customer feedback is going to be a good outlet for good and bad reviews to be left for the company site in some public area. The social presence of the company is going to have a significant impact on how the customers are eventually going to view the company in some cases, and this is why it is good to create a strong public presence. Having followers or obtaining likes on the account will be good for exposure, but having solid viewers that are going to come straight to your website by picking good word habits are better. These good word habits are going to be obtained when the company takes a look at Google Adwords. This company is a service provider of word generations that are calculated by traffic on the web that viewers leave to servers everywhere. Having viewers come to the account with a relatable topic on their mind before they arrive as new customers, they are going to be comfortable when they follow through to drop a couple of things into their shopping carts to purchase. Customers feel appreciated when they are greeted by custom messages in their notification box, or even offered shipping coupons that can discount shipping costs or purchases for loyalty rewards. Look for ways to amaze your customer so that they feel more user-friendly to the environment that you are making if you have a selling platform website. The style of how to put products that you are going to sell is going to be another vital role that is going to make up the selling world. Do right by using the FBA company but also utilize Google Adwords alongside to create a greater form of communicative marketing to the customers that are surrounding you. There are many domains a company can own depending on how many monthly charges they want to pay for a month, and having unlimited domains would mean that your chances of someone finding your website off of a miscalculated surf will still end up more than 40% increase in viewers coming to the site to see if it is the site. There are flow charts on these service provider sites that are going to help you see the frequency of the site's traffic. Pay attention to the specific things that the customers do on the websites, and make sure that you can trace any of their steps as you are the customer. This is going to help your web developer fully optimize the company site to be easier for users to navigate if there are a lot of destinations. These strategies are going to make it so much easier to expose the company name to well-recognized words and phrases so that the company will have an easier time becoming a more common outlet. Personalize every single order that is being sent out to make the customer feel as the company will stand out from the rest. Be sure to acknowledge the customer when they are coming to your website, and send notifications to the loyal customers that deserve an extra reward for always showing loyalty through purchasing through the company site. Having a strong connection with the customers that are interested in keeping up with company forums is going to create groups of sophisticated followers that will be purchasing your products and services for their personal end of the cut later. Customers are going to want to be addressed by their name especially on return slip statements if things do not go as planned for the shipment, but even these means of personalizing a customer's interaction with the company is going to lead the rapport of the company far.

Having great rapport with your customer is going to be crucial for easier customer requests to be made and fulfilled. The company needs to welcome their customers, making a clear point and possible support page to contact and receive purchasing and shipping support. Make a center where the customer is going to be able to communicate with the seller for the items in the shopping carts. For certain product information, make a point to include further contacting information or any research information that the customer is going to need to look further into the issue. When making the listing that the customer is going to see, make sure to include personal product information and any details that come with the products. Make a great product description so that it can further entice the customer to purchase the product even though they may have never purchased before and they are wary of their spending.

Chapter 9: Get Started with Retail Arbitrage

Retail arbitrage is going to translate a whole new type of selling experience in the world of the consumer. This world of selling is going to establish deep connections between companies everywhere and put the sale on the front lines of the audiences on the internet. These sales are going to change the way that we view products and what products are going to be trending when the rest is left over. This ever-changing market of commerce is going to show us that the trending products aren't always going to rule over the fiscal market. Products are going to be able to come and go, but it is at the responsibility of the company owner to find a way to diversify old and new products alike. Old products are not necessarily sold out because we must remember that there are customers out there that are looking for good quality products that are also marked down for a better cost. These customers are going to find our product listings and see the value that we have, keeping a strong market value of the products we do choose. There may be thousands of vendors that could possibly have the same products in your inventory right now, but there needs to be a strategy implemented to shine above all of the rest so that companies approach you to supply their demand. Adjusting price points every quarter is going to be a positive trending routine as it will always be a constant matching point for any other companies that are offering the same types of products or services. This is the perfect time to step in with new goals that separate the company's values from the rest. The company has to run a simple and efficient plan for all of their customers and it doesn't necessarily need to be this new wave that sweeps the nation.

The customers are looking for simple and reliable shipping with their good products and that is going to ultimately make the customer happy.

Selling OA is going to be a journey that one is going to have to experience on their own to learn the ins and outs, but there are consultants that one can hire to get a more in-depth dive on how to fully sell to the fullest potential. There is going to be great profits if the company can stay aware of the prices and rates that surround them in their current times, because as long as they can stay ahead with other companies making these sales, they will be able to rack up great customer traffic that helps them establish a great name of the business while ramping up. There are going to be possibilities for some of the clients of the consumer going to approach the company in new lights. Maybe there will be another company that wants to join the partnership in some way or form, and this is going to be the moment when there are thoughts about the future and where the company sees itself in the years to come. Do not fear these new endeavors because some of them are going to be time-sensitive and you should definitely jump on future profits if the numbers have been ran that it is going to be a positive gain. There are going to be companies that want to step in for partnership that also might ask you to sell their white-labeled products or vice versa, where you will purchase white-labeled products and distribute them exclusively to other vendors. White product labeling is going to be a great starting point to selling really good quality at affordable rates and being able to market to these audiences is going to be crucial for the price points that the company sets each quarter. The company is going to pull in great margins with selling white label products because they are not going to come with an expensive brand name to weight down the customer. The customer is going to have to trust in the product that the company provides by seeing that it has a strong presence on selling sites or other providers that can include social media. These broadcasts are going to be good for the company to get a spotlight somewhere in the community. The individual company may just be flipping wholesale, but it will still be good to have a strong presence for anyone that is looking to use your services, or if there are customers that want to refer others to you. It is not always necessary but we recommend that if the company can make a website for the shop and can do so by downloading WordPress and the proper plugins, they will be able to utilize their selling space online to drive the customers to the right areas and to make the right sales. This is going to be good for anyone who needs to contact for location or emergency shipment contact because information can be left on a specific page for the customer to find and be directed.

This is going to play directly into using a tool like Google Adwords and with this tool, there is going to be an optimization of the company site and links all across the internet. Adwords will be able to allow the consumer to track all of the important and frequently searched words on the Google database, and help decipher which ones are being currently looked at and how much traffic they are going to drive in on a regular basis. Making sure that your keywords are going to shine is important when the customer is opening up a browser to search the name. If it is not a well-known name, the company is going to suffer by having customers miss their page or indirectly landing on another page that is not similar in any way. The optimized keywords are going to give a better idea of what the customer sees when they first search for something like your company. These keywords are important to also think about when you are going to post listings for the products in the inventory. Posting really good listings is going to take more than just the simple product knowledge. The customer is going to be satisfied with this information but they are also going to need some personalization to go with it so it ensures them that when they finally purchase the product, they are really doing something for them and that is the great feeling to have. Keywords are going to bring the customer that much closer to you when they search your name in the search bar. Good keywords are also going to make sure that your ads are going to pop up correctly for the right customers. Creating better listings now that you know about the power in Adwords, there can be a custom listing made that is designed to make it easier and more relevant when the customer may see an ad that was their last week's inquiry. Be open to change if you can accept that it is going to optimize the assets of the company for the better. It is a changing online world and we are always going to change our ads and our listings for the better. There are going to be customers that are already used to our listings and we are going to need to go that extra mile to make a posting that is going to keep even our veteran customers still engaged.

Products are going to be the main value of the shop so we must remember to have a good selection and of great quality, if we want our customers to come back or to refer some of their friends. When selling OA, you get a lot of chances to choose the types of products that you do want. Although there are a ton of markets that are going to have the products that you need, it is going to be essential that a proper product search is going to be conducted to find the right fit for the market you are opening. Products come from far around the world to source the proper distributors, and it is going to be one of the main steps to be able to pick a product out to buy in. These products can be anything and the only other factor that needs to be thought of is the quantity. The company is going to need to get the best bang for their buck if they are looking to resell the goods and make out with any profit in the end. There needs to be budgeting and selling strategy made up with an FBA account and there can be profits calculated using the tools in FBA. Think logistically about the purchase move that is going to be made because the company might end up sitting on the products for quite some time before selling them all and this is going to be important.

Pick a product that has a great turn around rate so that there are no dull moments in quarterly income. Products that sell year-round are going to be good for the common customer, but we need to make sure that we sell a product that has the proper weight and price distributions. We need to sell the right product because we need to remember that we pay fees for using these types of services. There are going to be listing fees and even transactional fees for the products that are going to be sold on these accounts. It is important to have a plan in order once the product is being purchased so that the company can keep the account and still be able to hold onto further inventory if they are not making any sales during a dry period. Have a plan together for the profits the company does make and consider reinventing this money back into the business to ramp up production to be doubled. If this process can be done correctly, there is going to be a changeup in the budgeting system as well in the marketing systems. There is going to be more inventories in the warehouse and this is going to mean that extra orders can be made to gain that marginal income. Extra products on the shelves are going to be a perfect time to make another shipment that can be large to take away excess inventory that can make room for new products. These new deals can be discounted for new customers if you are dealing with new leads, and these products could be sold at newly prorated amounts. Once the company has been selling a product strong, it will be the next step to add more products into the inventory. The inventory is going to grow, especially if the company makes personal relationships with their clients. They are going to get to know more and more of the customer concern or urges and this is going to make it easier to list products and order things that the customer has spoken of. There are even going to be customers that come to the shop and they are going to ask for custom orders on shipping rates or product options that they are curious of, and it is your job to optimize their experience in the best way possible. Custom orders from clients are going to be some of the most well-paid in the business considering that it is custom made fit for them and the fact that it is going to be so hands-on for the company delivering. Purchase more products for the product line and make great listings about them that are going to relate to each other to tell a story of quality about the company.

The products that you represent on FBA are either going to be picked from Amazon's warehouses or they are going to be of the company's choice. These products are going through Amazon, regardless through FBA and this means that there needs to be complete compliance and the utmost representation when selling through the platform. Amazon will give percentage points to the companies that are selling their products because they like to market directly through affiliation when things can be purchased through third-party dropshippers. This is the perfect time to step in and represent them with the best quality and show the customers how your products are just an extension of Amazon and you are also a strong shop that is looking for more traffic. You may not want to advertise the company on a third-party hosting program like FBA, but there are plenty of ways that you can include the message of the company by creating a solid connection with the community that purchases your product. Creating messages to the customer and reaching out to them when they least expect it is going to build some of the stronger traits a company will have with customer interaction. Customer interaction time is going to be important for the consumer to finally tap into the "wants and needs" of the customer. Not every customer is going to blatantly tell you exactly how they come to expect a product arrival or a processing fee to drop and affect their bank account. In turn, these customers can be informed and educated about the processes the company will have, and they can make great interactions with the customers that are going to teach them how to fish rather than give them a free paper of fish and chips. Get to know the customer by reaching out and getting some of their personal information. If they are a frequent shopper or becoming one, then get some information and enroll them into a rewards program that allows them to earn rewards on the purchases made with the company. Cut better deals for the clients that turn long-term and make sure they know how much they mean and how you are going to give back to their loyalty. Sending welcoming messages and welcoming the customer to join forums about products or mission development within the company is going to connect a certain type of viewer to the company, and these viewers are going to be interested in the news that comes about. These viewers are the ones that we will invite to the press conference when we launch our first accolades. Engage every type of viewer simply by optimizing their communication with the site. If you are shipping out three thousand units yesterday, then be sure to send a message the night before to the receiver and inform them that they will be receiving their shipment soon. Make sure the customer knows that you care and they will always come back for more even if you are troubleshooting their package failure. Just create helpful hints and easy-to-navigate pages on the sites or Seller Central so that the customer has the easiest time coming in and out to grab exactly what they were looking for. Create a support center or page that the customers are going to come to for any concerns and this is going to be a place to receive even further opportunities that can include partnerships that can be made with other founders or creators. Having a healthy communication factor for the company is going to be an essential key to having a fully revolutionized shop. Most customers are just looking for a place to feel comfortable and to have all of their questions answered when they are purchasing things that they will use every day.

Trust these selling providers to take care of you and the welfare of the business as long as there are mutual investments. The more you can invest with the company is going to make up the better success that is going to happen when the FBA teams see that you are engaging the system more and giving back to FBA more with these goals. MCF centers are going to be a strong start for a shop to start shipping their products out, but it is not going to be the only option when considering that there are other needs that the consumer needs to fulfill. The provider is going to help fulfill the needs of these customers by supplying customer support and time-fulfillment. They are going to even print out shipping labels if there is no system in place to do it otherwise. Pick a reliable source like Amazon FBA to conduct business through their professional selling accounts to jump-start the company with a low budget. This low budget will double if proper care is taken when considering the selling fees and listing fees that will cost the company site time to fulfill. Assuming that you don't own the warehouse, we are going to accomplish so much more from the press of a button rather than we would by managing the physical shipping center and inventory warehouse. Trusting the company to conduct quality control is going to be a concern that many companies have about their products going in and out for shipment. It is good to get a system in place for packages to be checked for quality before they are sent off for shipment in case there are any misguided packages or tampered package slips. This is going to be important for the company to have routine checks so that there are no ill concerns or thoughts that leave the buyer feeling like they are helpless without an answer. Give your customers' answers by utilizing tools through Amazon FBA that will help you stay in touch with the customer and keep them engaged with the products that they are ordering. It is important to have the customers know how important their shipping is and also how important their business is, so make a point to reach out with FBA and give some kind words that let your customer know that you appreciate them. Amazon FBA is going to uphold a great reputation that is going to give your customer's a great comfortability to be able to ask questions to you. Think about all the customers that go to Amazon already as trusted customers and this is going to give you a projection of customer influx to the company with other tools that can read inflow of viewers. Tools like this are going to include Google Adwords, and they are going to be used to track the popular terms and words that the viewers are using to obtain traffic results. This tool, in particular, can help a company to make calculated decisions on the products that they are purchasing and the add listings that they are releasing on these products every quarter. Good ads are going to be vital to viewers who are actually going to take a look at these products, minding that there are companies out there that do not have quality listings and they rely on cheap products that can easily ship out to customers that are in a different demand. Not every customer is going to be looking for quality and they may only need to fulfill the needs of their customers through adequate quantities. This is going to be important when picking the products that go onto the sites. Diversity is important when the product line is going to overall make decisions, whether the company is going to pick up a unit or a pair. Some products are going to be more high-end than others and by listing these expensive products, it is going to become a great source for those that are willing to dish out the money. These products are going to be arbitrage at a better value for you, so there will be sales made as long as the customer knows they are also getting marked down and that the demand will meet the budget of the customer. In turn, there are going to be customers that are coming to the site with a set budget to spend and they are going to see if your products have what it takes to fulfill the financial means of the company. These products are going to be sold at lower values and they are going to be offered in great quantities if the seller is willing to list that much inventory. Creating this ramp up in production is going to allow more customers to purchase the items and there might even be a great turn around for viewers coming in to get these same deals. Good values are going to drive a lot of customers to purchase in the shop because they know that there are only a few distributors around that are going to provide them the same satisfaction. Look at the trends that are going to give you the quarterly progress to make these sales monthly, and figure out the right hot spot for the customers that are coming for value, quality, and efficiency. When there is one hundred percent satisfaction for the customer, they are going to become an integral part of the business once you create the selling plans with them. Once you finalize product orders for scheduling and once there are returning customers, we can start to decide where we are going to put our profits whether it is to resell extra inventory to the customers, or if it is to optimize the orders that are being placed with the current customers.

Revenue Tracking

The only way you are going to be able to track expenses and business spending is through creating a budget that is specifically designed for the company income. A budget is a monthly money plan and it is going to represent all of the expected and earned income into several categories that are going to be for the whole month or quarter. Make sure that the income that is rolling is going to be equal to the monthly expenses. Record every expense that goes in and out of the company, and make sure to track these things electronically or by writing them down and one can even make copies of the PO's and receipts that they are making with the business conducted. Watch and track these amounts and find how they are going to affect every category that makes up the business budget. Keep a calendar that is going to track every expense that was made and on the day of. This tracking can also be done by listings day to day spending that will show on every single day. Watch these expenses to also note all of the gains that are going to be made within the next possible quarters. These numbers are going to become timeline proof about the income and earnings that can be gathered every month in business. These budgeting tools are going to help predict the future of the company spending. The company is going to need a great vision of where they are going to end up when they acquire more and more assets. Put all of the information on a spreadsheet and organize everything to the rolling calendar days so that profits and losses can be documented as they happen. Create spreadsheets that you can send to customers or partners that are going to be part of the business. This is going to make a strong impact on the partners that are going to stand close-knit to the customer to be able to make calculated moves that are going to market the values and products of the company. Create interactive guides that are going to let a company look into the attributes of the company and what sales are going to drive the revenue towards. Before you go into business with a partner that you are engaging new ties in, feel free to show them how you are going to help their company shine and this could be with spreadsheets and sales graphs. Track revenue and be in front of all of the budget decisions because the savings that are wasted by spending is going to be noticed by next month. It is only so long until the budget will begin to take special hits towards the policies that need to be funded but are failing. Tracking the revenue is going to make a plan for the company that is interchangeable depending on spending and this is going to create a bigger market value that is going to be monitored and implemented when the planned attach is underway. Hiring an accountant is going to be a great step to take when managing the finances that it takes to run the shop. The accountant can have the responsibility of revenue tracking and creating better budgets and these tasks are going to fall onto their shoulders, so it is important to accept someone who is ready for every aspect of the work. Track everything down to business expenses and make sure to note the things that the company is going to use in the office or outside for business purposes. These tactics are going to make a greater return during tax season when you get the return you deserve on the necessities that are needed to conduct business, which may include shipping labels and boxes. This individual is going to meet up with the owner and have annual sales meetings that are going to display the current earnings of the company and where the company will be expecting to go. They will create bar graphs or pie charts and these diagrams are going to solidify all of the business being conducted for other viewers to see. If there are chairmen looking to take hold of the company and the assets, the accountant is going to be a great part of the team that is going to present the true value of their company with factual numbers.

Profit Banqueting

Sit on the profits that are made and we are saying this because there are a lot of companies out there that do not know where to stop investing their resources. If the startup budget is all the company has as a resource, then we need to hold tight to it so we do not waste it away on purchasing inventory we must sell for all the marbles. Design a strategy that will allow the company to purchase a product to flip, but as well hold a set amount of assets that the company can use in any case of company changes or inventory adjustment. It is going to be vital to set a nest egg for the company budget in case any emergency were to happen. There can be halts on service charges if the company is on automatic pay with their accounts and this is going to be crucial that the accounts and the balances are always being checked for constant buying privilege. Check every balance status to issue refunds for any customers that need and have a system in place for anyone that needs refunds to their banks or custom paying habits. The idea of profit banqueting is going to keep a solid system in place for people that are trying to make capital gains and not use the money that comes from the business to personal. This kind of money mentality is going to create a great saving routine for the companies that are trying to optimize their selling market and increase their inventory count. Use strategy when saving the money that is made, and make sure that the right account is being filled so that there are paper trails to every penny earned. This is going to be necessary when tax season rolls around and it will be time for annual returns. Profits are going to be just that and they are not going to translate sooner as spending money and this is an important note. The money earned can be used to flip the arbitrage and this is a necessary step but we cannot spend one hundred percent of the budget or profit, so we need to design a system that is always going to keep us grounded in our profit plans. Spend a percentage of the profit or budget when it is necessary, or when you are trying to purchase more inventory but never purchase with these funds if it is by all means not necessary. Make sure your accountant is going to be right there with you when you make the decisions to move money from one account to another. These precautions are going to be taken when the company is getting more ramped up for greater business. With more money that comes flowing into the business shop, the more precautions that are going to need to be taken. Earning more and more assets is going to create a sensitive system that needs to be under proper watch and tracking. This is why we recommend that the company use security tools for their privacy to protect any kind of information that the company owner has. These safety measures will also protect the information of the customers that leave their names and credit card numbers with our site to trust. SSL certificates for sites space and encrypted codes are going to be the way we protect this information but that is why we have great companies like Amazon. Through Amazon FBA, these service providers are going to be able to encrypt our products and our services so that others can enjoy our products without having to completely run a website or host our own shop. All money spent through these service providers is also going to go through third-party fee checking as a means of creating time stamps for PO's that roll through shopping carts. Having that extra care done for the sales that are made on these sites is going to be great for revenue tracking and it is going to make e-commerce simpler for the average seller. Minimizing the steps it's going to take to sell and ship products to the customers are going to create better, defined work steps taken to make the most out of the customer experience.

Recap

We have run through so many steps and this is a perfect time to recap. When we are stepping into the world of selling OA, we are going to make haste for the care we have to put into the products we are selling. Through retail arbitrage, companies have the potential to make quick profits with a little to no startup cost. This is going to be great for the individual that is looking to jump-start their new business, or if they are already engaged in a 40-hour work week and they are looking to make a passive form of earned income. We talked about ways we are going to automate a service provider to help us with every sale and transaction that needs to go through for every customer to have a chance to pick up our products up. We are going to find reliable suppliers that are going to be able to meet the demands of the customers on the other side. Developing these strong relationships with these distributors through wholesale accounts is going to create a better vision of where the company will purchase next, and this will also open a lot of doors to great deals on the products that are being purchased. When we first set up our first sale, it is most likely going to be through Amazon FBA and this is a great place to start to ensure that our customers will be able to purchase and they will be able to contact for customer support when necessary. One of the most important aspects of online sales is communication towards the customer and overall audience. These communication skills are going to lead the company to trustworthy sales and it is going to engage the customer into reading into the listings that are being posted. Customers should be able to read into the ad or listings and personally relate to them so that there can be urgency created to purchase through the company and to prioritize the values that are set forth. Be prepared for the amount of work you will be stepping into because it is not going to be as simple as two clicks and done. Although the world of selling retail arbitrage is becoming easier and easier as the years go on, that still doesn't mean that the owner of the business will be able to just sit back and collect a check. There is a need to put an effort and at times, the hard work that is shown is going to amount to the company's worth. Make sure that all of the steps taken are for the better future of the customers and this is going to ensure that these customers are going to come back and make purchases as dedicated buyers.

Conclusion

A good company is going to start with a great business model and this is going to revolve around the customers that are in front. Mission statements are going to be remembered by the customer, whether they read it or not, and this is true for all of the sellers that have personal interactions with their customers. Having a good ethic to put the customer first at all times is going to make the customer feel special every time they come and visit the shop. This can be done by simple means of acknowledgment and even addressing customers with their names is going to drive good responses back to the site if it is genuine. When the products are being purchased for the shop shelves, remember that there are more than a few sources out there to obtain fulfillment. There are going to be plenty of products to choose from, and one of the easier options will be able to participate in Amazon FBA, which will allow the consumer to choose from an even bigger variety of products. There is going to be a lot of diversity for these products, but buying and selling are not going to be that easy. The company is going to need to enroll through FBA to sell on the platform and with this, will come a few fees, which will include shipping fees and listing fees. Purchase products through wholesale distributors to make bigger profits on these platforms so that you can stay ahead with a great profit routine.

2019 is going to bring a lot of promise to any company that is flipping OA with its resources today. This year will show all of us how to make an easier sale and that it can be through companies like Amazon that represent our products with the utmost reputation. When it comes to Multi-Channel Fulfillment, the selling will be the same but there won't be the same support systems that are offered to the customer by FBA. This is going to be a decision a company makes when they decide to sell through these sites but keep their listed products off lists. This is okay too, but we always need to consider that with every sale that is going to be made, there will be follow up and communication to practically all of the customers that are supporting us. Keep a great communicative relationship open to the customers that are coming to purchase, because this is going to be a great factor that brings these customers back knowing they have a healthy and comfortable experience when they do come. Sales are becoming different to make in the states as well as the surrounding territories for the platforms to operate. Companies are going to be able to make new decisions for their selling shops rather than having to own retail shops that have physical address for customers to come into. Instead of paying tax and fees on the warehouse that is going to store the products, the company can rely on Fulfillment centers like that with Amazon. These centers are going to house the products in the online inventory and they are going to pack, label, and ship the products that the owner picks and lists. This is going to provide less responsibility for the company and it will free up a lot of time and effort that the company can use to calculate their future steps. If someone has extra time on their hands, then they should start the accounts and check out the fees of the providers to see if it is going to be a profitable change to the routine the profits are flowing in. It is recommended to make the first order and try shipping the first one out to see how it feels for the first time. These products are going to need to get out there for the customers and they are waiting to see. Customers are not going to find out that you are around their corner if you do not post that great listing. Take your chance with retail arbitrage and find your niche because it may just become the new norm.

www.ingramcontent.com/pod-product-compliance
Lightning Source LLC
Chambersburg PA
CBHW060856170526
45158CB00001B/378